LEADING WITH EXCELLENCE

5 Incredibly Useful Leadership Insights
From 100 Top Achievers

RAAM ANAND et. al.

STARDOM BOOKS

STARDOM BOOKS

WORLDWIDE

www.StardomBooks.com

STARDOM BOOKS

A Division of Stardom Publishing

and infoYOGIS Technologies.

105-501 Silverside Road

Wilmington, DE 19809

Copyright © 2019 by Stardom Publishing.

All rights reserved, including right to reproduce this book or portions thereof in any form whatsoever.

FIRST EDITION JANUARY 2019

Stardom Books
Leading with Excellence/ 5 Incredibly Useful
Leadership Insights From 100 Top Achievers

Raam Anand et. al.

p. cm.

Category: Self-help/Leadership

ISBN-13: 978-1-7934080-0-6

DEDICATION

This book is dedicated to all those amazing souls who had the guts and perseverance to overcome the insurmountable challenges that life threw at them and survived successfully to tell their stories of struggles, successes and triumphs, in this book. No wonder it's called "Leading with Excellence!"

DISCLAIMER

The views, opinions and information presented in this book are from the invited contributors of the publication. The publisher does not endorse or subscribe to the information; reader discretion is solicited.

This book is designed to provide information on how each one of the contributors did what they did, as their own personal narrative. It is sold with the understanding that neither the contributors nor the publisher is engaged in rendering legal, accounting or other professional services. If legal or other professional advice is warranted, the services of an appropriate professional should be sought. Also, this book cannot be an exhaustive and complete presentation on the topics within the book. While every effort has been made to make the information presented here as complete and accurate as possible, it may contain errors, omissions or information that was accurate as of its publication but subsequently has become outdated by marketplace or industry changes or conditions, new laws or regulations, or other circumstances.

Neither the contributors nor the publisher accepts any liability or responsibility to any person or entity with respect to any loss or damage alleged to have been caused, directly or indirectly, by the information, ideas, opinions or other content in this book. If you do not agree to these terms, you should immediately return this book for full refund.

Note from the Publisher

It was a great pleasure to work with all the CONTRIBUTORS of this book to bring out their stories, perspectives and insights on how they did what they did.

Each one of them have gone through their own struggles, overcome challenges and successfully steered their businesses and careers into becoming a well-known name in their respective industries.

Through this publication, I wanted to bring out their views so that you, the reader can benefit and get inspired by their insights. The experts were specifically asked to share how they did what they did and their message to the world.

So, here it is, for not just your reading pleasure, but also as a reference guide to help you shorten the learning curve and outshine in your own personal endeavors.

As you are going to learn by reading from the contributors of this book, you will understand that all of them have one common thing to say… TAKE ACTION.

Go ahead, read the book, take action and bring about a positive difference in your life, business and career – today!

WHEN YOU ARE RIGHT AND OTHERS ARE WRONG...
-- BE FORGIVING AND CONSIDERATE
WHEN YOU ARE WRONG AND OTHERS ARE RIGHT...
-- BE APOLOGETIC AND COURAGEOUS
..BECAUSE IT TAKES A LOT OF COURAGE TO BE SORRY AND APOLOGIZE.

Raam Anand, Publisher.

CONTENTS

QUESTION #1: ONE BOOK THAT YOU RECOMMEND A YOUNG LEADER TO READ......................................1

QUESTION #2: ONE ONLINE RESOURCE YOU RECOMMEND FOR SOMEONE JUST STARTING..........17

QUESTION #3: YOUR ONE PIECE OF ADVICE FOR SOMEONE WHO LOOKS UP TO YOU.........................33

QUESTION #4: WHO ARE/WERE YOUR ROLE MODELS THAT HAVE INFLUENCED YOU IN YOUR LIFE/BUSINESS/CAREER?...59

QUESTION #5: WHAT IS YOUR MESSAGE (IN ONE PARAGRAPH) TO THE WORLD?......................................87

ACKNOWLEDGMENTS

You have seen them often. You pick up a book and get to this section, and find that the author, once again, has dedicated the book to someone else and not you. Some unknown, non-existent assistant or some casual reference to famous people.

Not this time.

I would like to thank YOU for taking time to get this book. I would be even more grateful if you read the book and take ACTION to further your life and create a positive difference.

[FREE BOOK] - Get a free copy of our other book "Write Now" by Raam Anand, and see how you too can become a bestselling author EVEN if you have never written anything before!

Own book is the #1 marketing strategy used by successful and highly respected leaders all over the world. You too can become an author and create 10x better opportunities for your life and business.

Don't miss this one!

Click below or visit and claim your free copy before it's too late (just cover s&h, get it shipped to anywhere in India):

http://StardomBooks.com

Even though the results of becoming an author is incredible, writing a book can be a frustrating, painful process... especially if it's your first time. Raam has watched people struggle through this process (for years) the hard way, and he has also taught 1,000's of people to breeze through this process the easy way. Which way will you choose?

Here Are A Few Of the Things You'll Learn Inside This FREE Book...

+ Why should I write a book right now? - pg. 1

+ How a book turns attention into MONEY and how to create it FAST? - pg. 11

+ 6 Goals for writing a book and how to choose the BEST one? - pg. 27

+ How to become an author EVEN if you are not a professional writer - pg. 33

+ Creating a bestselling book EVEN if English is NOT your first language - pg. 39

+ My SECRET strategy for BUSY people who do not have time to write a book - pg. 43

+ Everything you should know about ISBN and why you should care about it? - pg. 47

+ Why shouldn't you SELF-PUBLISH your book (if you ignore this it will take you YEARS to write your book!) -pg. 51

+ How to choose what to WRITE about in your first book? (this insight can save you a lot of embarrassment later) - pg. 59

+ Who will read your book? this tip alone will help you start right and keep you from writing a book that no one reads! -pg. 63

+ Figuring out how much knowledge or wisdom is REALLY required for writing a book -pg. 67

\+ Using your book as a MARKETING weapon (HINT: the real returns from a book are in the back-end!) -pg. 75

\+ How to choose the RIGHT coach to help you become an internationally published author -pg. 83

\+ How to earn maximum ROYALTIES from your book (the wrong publisher choice can set you up for a huge loss) - pg. 91

\+ Why should I publish RIGHT NOW (don't let this chance slip through your fingers) -pg. 93

\+ Choosing whether to publish locally or going for a WORLDWIDE release (giving wings to your message) -pg. 136

\+ How to build your own EXPERT-EMPIRE around your thoughts using a book? - pg. 117

\+ How to use a book to start or grow your professional speaking career -pg. 119

\+ Self-Assessment - goal attainment and neuro-science based test on whether you can actually become an author! - pg 135

Here's What to Do Next...

Like I mentioned before, this book is FREE. All we ask is that you cover the small shipping and handling fee of just ₹49 only to get this book delivered to your address.

Get your free copy here:
http://StardomBooks.com

QUESTION #1
ONE BOOK THAT YOU RECOMMEND A YOUNG LEADER TO READ

Hopping over the Rabbit Hole: How Entrepreneurs Turn Failure into Success
by Anthony Scaramucci
Chandni Jafri, Founder and ED, SLSV (Sound and Light Social Ventures)

Monk who sold the Ferrari
Partha Chakraborty, GM Strategic Alliances

Any book on Emotional Intelligence
by Daniel Goleman
Poornima Bushpala,
Vice President Operational Risk & Control, Wells Fargo EGS India

Chanakya Niti
Vineet Kumar, Vice President - Talent Acquisition

Leading Apple with Steve Jobs
Dr. Sunil Pandey, Director (IT),
I.T.S, Ghaziabad

The Art of The Start 2.0 - Guy Kawasaki
Ish Anand, Founder - ReliaSmart Learning Systems Pvt. Ltd. (Business Doctors India)

Tuesdays with Morrie
Tushaar Kohli, Director SUN Group

"Who Moved My Cheese"
Lakshmiprasad Mhankali, Head of MIS & IT

"Celebrating Silence
by Sri Sri Ravi Shankar"
Rohit Kilam, Head Technlogy, Digital

"The Seven Habits of Highly Effective People"
by Stephen Covey
Sunil Sonare, General Manager at Sadbhav Engineering Limited

LEADING WITH EXCELLENCE

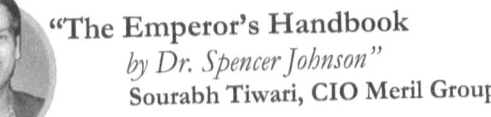
"The Emperor's Handbook
by Dr. Spencer Johnson"
Sourabh Tiwari, CIO Meril Group

"Playing with Fire - Nasser Hussain, Seven Habits Of Highly Effective People" *by Stephen Covey*
Madhusudan Warrier, Director - Information Technology, IDFC AMC Ltd

"The Bhagvad Gita
by Swami Chinmayananda"
Ketan Dewan, Co-Founder & CEO

The future of almost everything
by Global change guru Patrick Dixon
Mandar Sahasrabudhe
Head of IT infrastructure APAC, TUV SUD

The Inner Game of Tennis
by Tim Galleway
Rajiv Burman Head HR APAC Kronos

Rich Dad Poor Da
Manav Sarin
Head Business Development

Extreme Ownership: How U.S. Navy SEALs and Win
Devendra Deshmukh, CEO & e-Zest Solutions

"You can win"
by Shiv Khera
Vikram Vij, - Sr. Vice President, Samsung R&D

The Art of Persuasion
Vinay Chataraju- VP Business Development - Ephysx Technologies

Intelligent Leadership *by John Mattone*
Sandeep Gupta, Director & National Spokesperson, Expert Nutraceutical Advocacy Council

Thinking, Fast and Slow
- Anupam Sarda, AVP Product Management, HighRadius

What Got You Here Will Not Get You There by Marshall Goldsmith
- Ruchira Garg, Director, India ERC & Business Partnering, Adobe

LEADING WITH EXCELLENCE

7 Habits of Highly effective people
Prakash Kumar, Head IT, BMW Group India

Everyday Greatness
by Stephen Cobey
Arpan Banerjee, Orion Consulting Services, CEO

Managing Radical Change
by Gita Piramal
Vijay Chaudhry, Executive Vice President, Bry Air Asia

Evenings with Morie
Sandhya Jathar, Head Learning & Leadership DBS bank India

The Alchemist by Paulo Coelho
Chetan Swaroop, AVP, Pierian Services Pvt Ltd

Losing My Virginity
Rajarshi Datta, CEO, The CFO Centre India

Leadership and Self Deception
by Arbinger Institute
John Cherian, - Co-Founder & CEO

What your CEO wants you to know
Joy Banerjee, SVP & Head Learning and Development

Inside the C-Suite: 21 Lessons from Top Management to Get Your Way in Business and in Life
Ashish Mathur, Vice President &ValueFirst Digital

THE LEADER WHO HAD NO TITLE
by Robin Sharma
Harsha Parthasarathy, Chief Executive Officer @ Sellcraft Global Solutions

Chanakya's 7 Secrets of Leadership
By Radhakrishnan Pillai & D. Sivanandhan
Dr. Makarand Sawant, Senior General Manager - IT at Deepak Fertilisers And Petrochemicals Corp. Ltd.

An Autobiography of Steve Jobs
Sudhir Gouda, Head || Strategic Alliances - Angel Broking Limited

Hit Refresh
By Satya Nadella
Dr. Pramod Sadarjoshi, Founder & CEO, Talentsmith Consulting

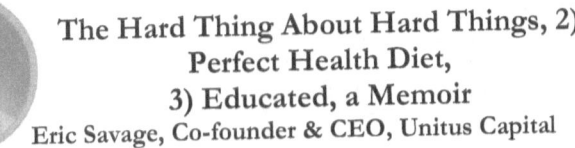

The Hard Thing About Hard Things, 2) Perfect Health Diet, 3) Educated, a Memoir
Eric Savage, Co-founder & CEO, Unitus Capital

Originals by Adam Grant
-Ghanshyam Ghanshyam Singh,
Director Supply Chain Management & Quality Assurance at Chai

Zero to One
by Peter Thiel
Anil Mishra, - CSS Corp

The Go-Giver Leader
by Bob Burg and John David Mann
Sanjay Mahajan, Chief Information Officer ||
Satin Creditcare Network Ltd.

Primal Leadership: Learning to Lead with Emotional Intelligence
by Daniel Goleman, Richard E. Boyatzis, Annie McKee
Rajalingam R, Founder Director & CEO,
Aberame Creative Solutions Private Limited

Adventures of a Curious Character
Srinath Gururaj Rao, Vice President | CHRO | Nexval Group

Jonathan Livingston Seagul
Sonal Jain, - HR Director
Johnson and Johnson

Good to Great
by Jim Collins
Saarthak Bakshi, CEO, International Fertility Centre

Outliers
Ramakrishna V
Head - HR, HFFC

Corporate Chanakya on Leadership
by Radhakrishnan Pillai
Sharmilaa Rajesh Kannan
Vice President Learning& Development

The Monk who sold his Ferrari
PK Shrivastava
Director- Fintech, Almoayed Technologies

The Leader who had no Title
Manoj Rawat
CEO, ValueFin India

Read Leaders Eat Last: Why Some Teams Pull Together and Others Don't
VARTUL MITTAL
Keynote Speaker - Technology & Innovation
- Ex IBM, Kotak Mahindra Bank, Coca Cola

SITA
by Amish
Arvind Chaudhary, Co Founder at passivereferral

Leadership and Self-Deception
Maniraj Juneja, Partner, Amitojeindia

Prelude to Foundation
by Issac Asimov
Sandipan Chattopadhyay, CEO and MD, Xelpmoc Design and Tech Limited

Play to Win
Rakesh Bhambhani
Chief Business Officer
Clove Technologies Pvt Ltd

8 Steps to Innovation: Going from Jugaad to Excellence
by Rishikesha T. Krishnan
Venkatachalam P
Chief People Officer of Monocept Consulting

Your Erroreous Zones
by - Dr Wayne Dyer
Nihar Ranjan
CEO Flashdeal

Man's Search for Meaning
Pratik Shah
Global Head of Marketing, InstaReM

Power of Subconscious Mind
Punit Thakkar
Shivaami Cloud Services Private Limited

Strengths Based Leadership: Great Leaders, Teams, And Why People Follow
by Tom Rath and Barrie Conchie
V.P. Prabhakaran
CTO, InfoSecTrain

Blue Ocean Strategy
Onais Rafiq
CEO - Fork Media India

Elon Musk: Tesla, SpaceX, and the Quest for a Fantastic Future
Sharjeel Siddiqui
Head of Marketing | LogiNext

Magic of Thinking Big
Jayprakash Vasdewani
CEO, Latitude Technolabs Pvt ltd

How Will You Measure Your Life?
Subash franklin
StratSprint

Shoe Dog: A Memoir by the Creator of
Nidhin Chandra Mohan
Director, SayOne Technologies Private

Who moved my cheese
by Spencer Johnson
Pranav Shandilya
Founder and CEO- 12th July Ventures

Situational Leadership
Siddharth Hosangadi
Vice President - Sales, Uniphore Software Systems

Decline and Fall of the Roman Empire
by Edward Gibbon
Gauraav Thakar, QualityKiosk, Vice President

Be the elephant
by Steve Kaplan
Akshar Peerbhoy, COO - MAA Communications

7 Habits of Highly effective People
by Stephen Covey
Srivibhavan Balaram
Managing Director, Vocera
Communications India Pvt Ltd

Hit Refresh
by Satya Nadella
Krishna Prasad
Interaction One Solutions Private Limited

Ramayana
Srikanth Appana
Co Founder & CTO, ASAP

Good to Great
Praveen Kumar Kalbhavi
CMD & CEO - Novigo Solutions Inc

Wings Of Fire
by Abdul Kalam
Flight Lieutenant At Kishore
Chief Entrepreneurial Officer, Vidhya Sangha

Influence
Ashesh Shah
CEO - Fusion Informatics Limited

Mastery Manual
by Robin Sharma
Anjani Madhavi
Vice President - Envestnet | Yodlee

Start With Why & End With How !
Dhruv Pandey
CEO (Maxosys Limited)

How to win friends and influence people
by Dale Carnegie
Vikas Chadha
Executive Director and CFO Berggruen Hotels Pvt ltd

"The New Rules of Marketing & PR"
by David Meerman Scott
Kalyan Acharya
Business Development Head-Global Sales at Yudiz Solutions Pvt. Ltd.

Tribal Leadership
by Dave Logan, Halee Fischer-Wright, and John King
Madhuri Mandaogade
CEO, Humane BITS

Xiaomi Way
by Li Wanqiang
Manav Jeet
MD & CEO

Master of Opportunity and Make It Big
by Richard M. Rothman
Sachin Deshpande, Co-Founder & CEO

Lee Iacocca - An Autobiography
Chakravarthy Murugesan, General Manager, Net 4 India Ltd

LEADING WITH EXCELLENCE

The Secret
Amit Dua, CEO, Signity Solutions

The Innovator's Dilemma
by Clayton Christensen
Sankar Bora, Founder & COO @Dealshare

Shoe Dog
Hitesh Gossain, Managing Director, Onspon.com

Why
by Simon Sinek

Sanjaya Mariwala, Omniactive Health Technologies Ltd

ReWork Jason Fried and David Heinemeier Hansson
Romi Chugh, Founder - Ekon Solutions

To Sell Is Human
Gaurav Loria Group Chief Quality Officer & Head Administration

The Power of Now

Hoshang Vashisht
CEO at Vashisht Group of Companies

How to Get from Where You Are to Where You Want to Be: The 25 Principles of Success

Nagaraja Javvaji, AVP
Demand Generation & Cigniti Technologies

The Alchemist
by Paulo Coelho
Pankaj Sharma
V.P. Sales, Shaligram Infotech LLP

QUESTION #2: ONE ONLINE RESOURCE YOU RECOMMEND FOR SOMEONE JUST STARTING

Sandhya Jathar Head Learning & Leadership DBS bank India	HBR
Chetan Swaroop AVP, Pierian Services Pvt Ltd	https://bookboon.com/
Rajarshi Datta - CEO, The CFO Centre India	Google
John Cherian Co-Founder & CEO	www.inc42.com

Joy Banerjee **SVP & Head Learning and Development**	Flipboard and Blinkist
Ashish Mathur **Vice President &ValueFirst Digital**	Harvard Business Review
Harsha Parthasarathy **Chief Executive Officer @ Sellcraft Global Solutions**	Search for the best life coaches in your respective region, all are good.
Dr. Makarand Sawant **Senior General Manager - It At Deepak Fertilisers And Petrochemicals Corp. Ltd.**	Basic Skills in Management and Leadership - Free Management Library https://managementhelp.org/freebusinesstraining/leadership.htm
Sudhir Gouda **Head | Strategic Alliances - Angel Broking Limited**	Harvard business review & other platforms that teach you to focus, concentrate or meditate
Sachin Deshpande **Co-Founder & CEO**	**https://steveblank.com**

Chakravarthy Murugesan General Manager, Net 4 India Ltd	Carpe Diem - live the moment
Amit Dua CEO, Signity Solutions	Startup stories sites which motivates and inspires you to say yourself "Yes, I can and I will". Personally like yourstory.com
Sankar Bora Founder & COO @Dealshare	Coursera
Hitesh Gossain Managing Director, Onspon.com	Mashable
Sanjaya Mariwala Omniactive Health Technologies Ltd	Google
Romi Chugh Founder - Ekon Solutions	Slideshare - repository of great information

Gaurav Loria **Group Chief Quality Officer & Head Administration**	Amazon- Has A Great Library Of Reading Material
Hoshang Vashisht **CEO at Vashisht Group of Companies**	Entreprenuer
Nagaraja Javvaji **AVP Demand Generation & Cigniti Technologies**	- HBR.ORG
Arvind Chaudhary **Co-Founder at Passivereferral**	I being a non tech founder of a tech startup it's important to have basics of technology. During initial days I spent time on codacamy online and realized notepad is for writing codes and of course I learnt html ass and JavaScript later.
Srivibhavan Balaram **Managing Director, Vocera Communications India Pvt Ltd**	Susan David's website on Emotional Agility

Chandni Jafri **Founder And Ed, Slsv (Sound And Light Social Ventures)**	Ted talks
Partha Chakraborty **GM Strategic Alliances**	Anything better than google?
Poornima Bushpala **Vice President Operational Risk & Control, Wells Fargo Egs India**	Economic times, download the app and just don't read but apply critical and analytical thinking based on facts provided, also try to answer 'why'
Vineet Kumar **Vice President - Talent Acquisition**	Create a profile on LinkedIn& follow top influencers
Dr. Sunil Pandey **Director (It), I.T.S, Ghaziabad**	https://www.wikipedia.org

Ish Anand **Designation & Company - Founder - Reliasmart Learning Systems Pvt. Ltd. (Business Doctors India)**	Harvard Business Review
Tushaar Kohli **Director Sun Group**	Google
Dr. Pramod Sadarjoshi **Founder & CEO, Talentsmith Consulting**	Businessownerstoolkit.com
Ghanshyam Ghanshyam Singh **- Director Supply Chain Management & Quality Assurance At Chai Point**	Ted talks
Anil Mishra **CSS Corp**	www.forbes.com

Sanjay Mahajan Chief Information Officer | Satin Creditcare Network Ltd.	https://alltop.com/ and https://www.ted.com/talks
Rajalingam R Founder Director & CEO, Aberame Creative Solutions Private Limited	The brilliant failure of Steve Jobs (URL: https://www.huffingtonpost.com/william-bradley/the-brilliant-failure-of_b_8507632.html)
Srinath Gururajarao Vice President | CHRO | Nexval Group	Coursera.org
Sonal Jain HR Director Johnson And Johnson	LinkedIn
Saarthakbakshi CEO, International Fertility Centre	Business casual Youtube channel
Ramakrishna V Head - HR, HFFC	Hr.com

Sharmilaa Rajesh Kannan **Vice President Learning & Development**	Lynda.com
PK Shrivastava	Google with your brain!
Venkatachalam P **Chief People Officer Of Monocept Consulting**	Wharton school publications
Nihar Ranjan **CEO Flashdeal**	https://startupnation.com/start-your-business/entrepreneurs-share-start-business
Pratik Shah **Global Head Of Marketing, Instarem**	mashable.com
Punit Thakkar **Shivaami Cloud Services Private Limited**	startwithwhy.com

V.P. Prabhakaran CTO, Infosectrain	https://blog.asmartbear.com/
Pankaj Sharma V.P. Sales, Shaligram Infotech LLP	Subscribe to Tony Robbins, Gary Vaynerchuk, Simon Sinek, Sandip Maheswari
Manoj Rawat CEO, Valuefin India	Wikipedia
Vartul Mittal Keynote Speaker - Technology & Innovation - Ex IBM, Kotak Mahindra Bank, Coca Cola	www.hbr.org
Sandipan Chattopadhyay CEO And Md, Xelpmoc Design And Tech Limited	Github

Rakesh Bhambhani Chief Business Officer - Clove Technologies Pvt Ltd	Harvard business review
Sharjeel Siddiqui Head Of Marketing | Loginext	Openview labs has some really interesting articles on growth hacking
Jayprakash Vasdewani CEO, Latitude Technolabs Pvt Ltd	Do not have any specific resource. Try to connect with other entrepreneurs through LinkedIn
Subash Franklin Stratsprint	https://www.mentorbox.com
Nidhin Chandra Mohan Director, Sayone Technologies Private Limited	Harvard business review
Pranav Shandilya Founder And CEO - 12th July Ventures	LinkedIn

Siddharth Hosangadi **Vice President - Sales, Uniphore Software Systems**	LinkedIn
Gauraavthakar **Qualitykiosk, Vice President**	Google.com
Akshar Peerbhoy **COO - MAA Communications**	Susan David's website on emotional agility
Krishna Prasad **Interaction One Solutions Private Limited**	Slideshare - whole lot of stuff
Srikanth Appana **Co-Founder & CTO, Asap**	https://hbr.org
Flight Lieutenant At Kishore **Chief Entrepreneurial Officer, Vidhya Sangha**	For wireless professionals 3gpp.org; for software developers, ONAP

Ashesh Shah CEO - Fusion Informatics Limited	https://michaelhyatt.com/leadtowin/
Anjani Madhavi Vice President - Envestnet | Yodlee	Ted talks
Dhruv Pandey CEO (Maxosys Limited)	https://growthlab.com/3-weird-yet-successful-online-business-ideas
Vikas Chadha Executive Director And CFO Berggruen Hotels Pvt Ltd	LinkedIn to create your network
Kalyan Acharya Business Development Head-Global Sales At Yudiz Solutions Pvt. Ltd.	Resources from Hubspot give a lot of information about inbound marketing and sales
Madhuri Mandaogade CEO, Humanebits	There is no one particular source, you have to keep surfing through anything you can get your hands on

Lakshmiprasad Mahankali Head of MIS & IT	LinkedIn
Rohit Kilam Head Technology, Digital	Feedly
Sunil Sonare General Manager Sadbhav Engineering Limited	Reading of HBR
Sourabh Tiwari CIO, Meril group	The Alchemist
Madhusudan Warrier Director - Information Technology, IDFC AMC Ltd	Trends in Psychology - One of my favorites is https://www.socialpsychology.org/social.htm , https://www.learnpsychology.org/
Ketan Dewan Co-founder & CEO	Google
Mandar Sahasrabudhe Head of IT infrastructure APAC, TUV SUD	O365 products
Rajiv Burman Head HR APAC Kronos	hbr.org

Manav Sarin **Head Business Development**	The Secret
Devendra Deshmukh **CEO & e-Zest Solutions Ltd.**	HBR - Harvard Business Review
Vikram Vij **Sr. Vice President, Samsung R&D**	https://hbr.org/store/case-studies
Vinay Chataraju **VP Business Development - Ephysx Technologies**	Stanford GSB - Social Media Pages
Sandeep Gupta **Director & National Spokesperson, Expert Nutraceutical Advocacy Council**	www.johnmattone.com
Anupam Sarda **AVP Product Management, HighRadius**	Life is not fair, get used to it

Ruchira Garg **Director, India ERC & Business Partnering, Adobe**	HBR.org
Prakash Kumar **Head IT, BMW Group India**	Udemy
Arpan Banerjee **Orion Consulting Services, CEO**	https://scholar.google.co.in/

Manav Jeet **MD & CEO**	Wikipedia

QUESTION #3: YOUR ONE PIECE OF ADVICE FOR SOMEONE WHO LOOKS UPTO YOU

Lakshmiprasad Mahankali

Head of MIS & IT

Think Simple do not complicate & be Transparent

Rohit Kilam *Head Technology, Digital*	Meditate, Run, Sleep, Read and love what you do
Sunil Sonare *General Manager Sadbhav Engineering Limited*	Believe on facts and figure, do not be emotional. Believe on hard work.

Sourabh Tiwari *CIO, Meril group*	Reading is an essential life skill.
Madhusudan Warrier *Director - Information Technology, IDFC AMC Ltd*	Listen more and Talk when required. Never show off, Remain Humble. Share experiences and keep being better
Ketan Dewan *Co-founder & CEO*	Know the Self and follow the Self during fear, during anger and during desires. Then slowly all forms will drop and you will be clear Self.
Mandar Sahasrabudhe *Head of IT infrastructure APAC, TUV SUD*	Trust your capabilities, keep learning and honing your skills and be passionate about your work. Ensure to be innovative in approach and work with enthusiasm and positivity to succeed.

Rajiv Burman *Head HR APAC Kronos*	Make a long term plan for your life and ensure all your short term actions support that plan.
Manav Sarin *Head Business Development*	Give your best every day and think that it's the last day on earth
Devendra Deshmukh *CEO & e-Zest Solutions Ltd.*	Think with brain but act with heart
Vikram Vij *Sr. Vice President, Samsung R&D*	Don't get disgruntled by life's challenges..March on relentlessly, for every failure is a stepping stone to success. Believe in yourself. Learn from your mistakes. Think big. Think positive. Persistence and tenacity at the of adversity is what differenciates the leaders from the rest.

Vinay Chataraju *VP Business Development - Ephysx Technologies*	Be happy with what you have and never be satisfied with what you are.
Sandhya Jathar *Designation & Company - Head Learning & Leadership DBS Bank India*	Keep evolving and future relevant .. don't look at easy goals .. have BHAG goals
Chetan Swaroop *AVP, Pierian Services Pvt Ltd*	Travel as often as possible because the world is too big for you to stay in your comfort zone for too long.
Rajarshi Datta *CEO, The CFO Centre India*	Be passionate about what you do for a living

Sandeep Gupta *Director & National Spokesperson, Expert Nutraceutical Advocacy Council*	Fix your Purpose and go after it with Passion. And remember that your purpose to create impact on Heart, Soul and Mind of Society (People's Lives)
Anupam Sarda *AVP Product Management, HighRadius*	Life is not fair, get used to it
Ruchira Garg *Director, India ERC & Business Partnering, Adobe*	Focus on the problem you are trying to solve. If you get the problem statement right, the solution will be easier to find.
Prakash Kumar *- Head IT, BMW Group India*	Don't be afraid to try new things, in the you will only gain and learn.

Arpan Banerjee *Orion Consulting Services, CEO*	Enjoy whatever you are doing in your life and never lose focus
Vijay Chaudhry *Executive Vice President, Bry Air Asia*	Look for purpose in life and not for position. Position is always resultant.
John cherian *Co-founder & CEO*	Lots of people will give you advice, you are solely responsible for accepting the advice that is relevant for you and making it successful
Joy Banerjee *SVP & Head Learning and Development*	Always be open to learning and trying out new things, keep a growth mindset and most important is remain grounded

Ashish Mathur *Vice President & ValueFirst Digital*	Believe in yourself!
Harsha Parthasarathy *Chief Executive Officer @ Sellcraft Global Solutions*	"Always strive to do the right thing the first time" Its okay if you spend a little more time, but you can do wonders. Do your best, the best will definitely come to you".
Dr. Makarand Sawant *Senior General Manager - IT at Deepak Fertilisers And Petrochemicals Corp. Ltd.*	Built your own capabilities to manage any situation.
Sudhir Gouda *Head // Strategic Alliances - Angel Broking Limited*	Work as if you're the owner, Sell like it's your only meal, Plan like a general and Live like it's your last day.

Chandni Jafri *Founder and ED, SLSV (Sound and Light Social Ventures)*	Make learning, serving and empowering others your holy trinity.
Partha Chakraborty *GM Strategic Alliances*	You are never too old to reinvent yourself.
Poornima Bushpala *Vice President Operational Risk &Control, Wells Fargo EGS India*	Find your passion and create goals that could be achieved in short and long term. Try creating goals for every 3 to 5 years.

Vineet Kumar *Vice President - Talent Acquisition*	Do not follow anyone in your life, keep learning from others and create your own style of doing things with quality. Do not work for money, work to create a difference in someone's life by helping them. Money is by product of the good work you do and you won't have scarcity of it.
Dr. Sunil Pandey *Director (IT), I.T.S, Ghaziabad*	Understand your role, use your strength & work on your weaknesses, be passionate, focused, have self-belief and do your best. Success is yours.
Ish Anand *Founder - ReliaSmart Learning Systems Pvt. Ltd. (Business Doctors India)*	Be true to yourself, be passionate about what you do as that is what will make you happy and help you excel. Don't give a damn about what the world says!

Tushaar Kohli *Director SUN Group*	Just be a good human being .... It's the highest service to yourself and the world
Dr. Pramod Sadarjoshi *Founder & CEO, Talentsmith Consulting*	Be Passionate, purposeful, patient, prayerful, Productive & peaceful
Eric Savage *Co-founder & CEO, Unitus Capital*	The key to a successful "start-up" is "starting"
Ghanshyam Singh *Director Supply Chain Management & Quality Assurance at Chai Point*	Strive for excellence by being curious, questioning things, there is always scope for improvement, be it incremental or exceptional, this way you will add a lot of value to whatever work you take up and the world will be a better place because you came along!

Anil Mishra *CSS Corp*	Have a learning attitude and explore different roles as you build your career. Having a holistic understanding of the entire business gives you great confidence and growth.
Sanjay Mahajan *Chief Information Officer // Satin Creditcare Network Ltd.*	There is no shortcut to hard work & no compromise to Integrity. Positive Attitude & Collaboration is the key to success. Build Trust with the partners & exhibit strong business partnership approach.

Rajalingam R

Founder Director & CEO, Aberame Creative Solutions Private Limited

To be successful in life, you need to visualize the way you wish to live. Close your eyes and feel it that you accomplished your wish. Happiness is not something you can plan and get it later in life; it is something you need to find it in the present, it happens every moment. Believe it that you already got it. To be successful, you need to win your life along with money. A new world is open for you, NOW.

Srinath Gururajarao *Vice President / CHRO / Nexval Group*	Look up to me as your possibility in completing your pursuit as a hand being held firmly. Fulfilment for each individual including me comes from the core acceptance of co-existence and contribution towards completion of one another's pursuits towards a higher path. There no other better joy than this and as one moves ahead, so does one excel in this joy of holding and creating together.
Sonal Jain *HR Director Johnson and Johnson*	Your purpose is what you live for. Unfold it through experiences. Don't rush into it bit be like a traveller who enjoys every moment of the journey.

Saarthak Bakshi

CEO, International Fertility Centre

While finishing my Bachelors I became deeply committed to maximising every second and every opportunity that came my way. I started studying the self-improvement sections of libraries and bookstores. I knew what it was like to be easily distracted. I knew what it was like to go for social acceptance instead of following my own voice. I made a commitment to see what I was really capable of. At the end, I think all of us want more control and freedom in our lives. I knew that if I didn't control my pay check, I really didn't control my destiny. I want to show people that great things are possible. I want to show people that we can do other things besides be doctors, engineers & MBA grads. I wanted to let people know that you can share a positive message and create a life of meaning.

Ramakrishna V *Head - HR, HFFC*	Learn every day from everyone, you never know when it will come handy
Sharmilaa Rajesh Kannan *Vice President, Learning & Development*	There will be tough situations, bad days, rough patches in life, don't let them impact you. You are unique and your strength is not determined by hardships you faced but it is determined by your refusal to let those hardships change what you truly are. Be kind and humble, stand for what is right yet be tactful in dealing with conflicts, it goes long way in earning people. Make a difference in people's life, Thats all that matters when you are no more.
PK Shrivastava *Director- Fintech, Almoayed Technologies*	Always Focus on Big Picture, every problem has plenty of opportunities look for it and lastly plan to fail but never fail to plan.

Pradeep Kumar Cheruvathoor *Silence Global, Chief Inspiration Officer*	It is natural to search for happiness, but do not search for it outside you. It is your very nature
Pavan Verma *CEO - REDIAN SOFTWARE*	Success is not just earning the money, every milestone of life you complete is a success. Set pieces together and keep working towards your mission.
Venkatachalam P *Chief People Officer of Monocept Consulting*	Be yourself. Always be an Ethical and Value based person.
Nihar Ranjan *CEO Flashdeal*	The biggest hurdle you face will be in your early days, while you build the team. You will know, it's not easy at all. And if at all the team is built, making them stick together in the hard times of your journey will be the key.

LEADING WITH EXCELLENCE

Pratik Shah *Global Head of Marketing, InstaReM*	Work is a part of life, and not life. The sooner you realize this the better you'll be in all phases of your life, including work.
Punit Thakkar *Shivaami Cloud Services Private Limited*	The best place to find a helping hand is at the end of your own arm.
V.P. Prabhakaran *CTO, InfoSecTrain*	What you can dream, you can achieve
Pankaj Sharma *V.P. Sales, Shaligram Infotech LLp*	Consistency gives result and compound effect is true
Onais Rafiq *CEO - Fork Media India*	There is no alternative to hard Work.
Manoj Rawat *- CEO, ValueFin India*	Believe in it passionately and Pursue it Aggressively

Vartul Mittal **Keynote Speaker - Technology & Innovation - Ex IBM, Kotak Mahindra Bank, Coca Cola**	Read a lot as it brings you ahead of the learning curve than many who have been practicing things since ages but not doing them rightly.
Arvind Chaudhary *Co Founder at passivereferral*	Patience Consistency and continuous development is like paddling to make it keep moving
Manirajjuneja *Partner, Amitojeindia*	Work only on making other people's lives easier and the magic happens.
Sandipan Chattopadhyay *CEO and MD, Xelpmoc Design and Tech Limited*	Make yourself redundant.
Rakesh Bhambhani *Chief Business Officer - Clove Technologies Pvt Ltd*	Be Passionate, Be Objective and Keep it Simple

Sharjeel Siddiqui *Head of Marketing | LogiNext*	Follow a very simple formula - Understand, research thoroughly and validate your idea, concept, goal or vision that you set for yourself before your put in everything, remember, your time is more important than money.
JayprakashVasdewani *CEO, Latitude Technolabs Pvt ltd*	Just follow your heart. You will get lot of criticism, you will make mistakes, learn and grow from it. At times you will have your close relatives discourage you and give you examples of your peers doing really well. Remember what you are doing is not easy but journey will be worth it.
Subash Franklin *StratSprint*	Control the things which are in your control what you cannot control don't fret about it

Nidhin Chandra Mohan Director, SayOne Technologies Private Limited	Focus
Pranav Shandilya Founder and CEO - 12th July Ventures	Your life is the sum total of the choices that you take, so before making a choice; take a standalone call keeping yourself as the third person and then take the plunge. Remember, we make choices and don't look back.
Siddharth Hosangadi Vice President - Sales, Uniphore Software Systems	Become reliable.
Gauraav Thakar QualityKiosk, Vice President	There is nothing that the right team cannot solve. Build a great team because you win or lose together. Individuals contribute teams scale.
Akshar Peerbhoy COO - MAA Communications	Believe in yourself, and don't let anyone divert your own belief. Listen to the voice inside of you, 9 out of 10 times it is right.

Srivibhavan Balaram *Managing Director, Vocera Communications India Pvt Ltd*	Develop the growth mindset. Never be satisfied with what you know. Be a student all your life - never stop learning.
Krishna Prasad *Interaction One Solutions Private Limited*	Never be afraid of making a mistake or going wrong; be brave, its most often easy to say sorry than ask for permissions
Srikanth Appana *Co-Founder & CTO, ASAP*	1) Never ask anyone for advices and suggestions, build a quality and expertise to take decisions of your own. You should be master of your own. 2) Always learn from failures and disappointments, design a strategy to ensure these are not repeated again. 3) Believe in continuous learning, Academic learnings will just give you wings to take off, you need to keep learning to successfully fly and change wheels in the air on situations.

Praveen Kumar Kalbhavi *CMD & CEO - Novigo Solutions Inc*	Leadership is all about building a strong team around you.
Flight Lieutenant at Kishore *Chief Entrepreneurial Officer, Vidhya Sangha*	Doing Frugal Innovations by MORE emphasis on Indian Standards Developmental Work including likes of GISFI, TSDSI and fully exploit several aspirational missions of Government of India including National Super Computing Mission, 10000 START UPs warehouse by NASSCOM, Centre of Excellence on IoT. By 2020, India hopes to nurture 20,000 start ups
Ashesh Shah *CEO - Fusion Informatics Limited*	Think different, have fun, don't fear failure, Wear your enthusiasm and passion

Anjani Madhavi *Vice President - Envestnet | Yodlee*	Just focus on becoming incrementally better each day compared to the previous day... this is the secret to exponential growth!
Dhruv Pandey *CEO (Maxosys Limited)*	My Business Mantra for New Startups "Focus directs efforts efficiently" because focus is the cornerstone of any successful startup as well as focus helps build a strong product and solid business
Vikas Chadha *Executive Director and CFO Berggruen Hotels Pvt ltd*	Be patient, take your opportunities, take calculated risks in your choices, work hard there is no substitute for hard work.
Kalyan Acharya *- Business Development Head- Global Sales at Yudiz Solutions Pvt.Ltd*	Be an honest and a self-motivated sales person. Your prospects, clients and your company will really like you if you have these qualities and doing sales because of these qualities will get a lot easier for you.

Madhuri Mandaogade CEO, HumaneBITS	As an entrepreneur you can do anything, but not everything. Having a team with complementing skills is most important.
Manav Jeet MD & CEO	I am strong believer of 'Think big, dream big' mantra. Being an entrepreneur is an opportunity to disrupt and make a life changing difference. Every entrepreneur should make the most of this opportunity. And it can happen only when you aim high.
Sachin Deshpande Co-Founder & CEO	Collaboration, Business Networking and Giving it Back to Society !!
Chakravarthy Murugesan General Manager, Net 4 India Ltd	Believe in yourself.... for every Human Heart vibrates to that Iron string....
Amit Dua CEO, Signity Solutions	An organization is an impression of its leader. So, keep working to improve yourself - your positive spirits, your vision, your values and it will have an uplift effect on your organization/Startup.

Sankar Bora *Founder & COO @Dealshare*	Always be grounded and keep focusing on the learnings.
Hitesh Gossain *Managing Director, Onspon.com*	Think like a consumer and be very brutal with yourself and your assessments of yourself. Develop a key interest in sales - whatever your role maybe - as that innate ability will help you all across your professional life.
Sanjaya Mariwala *Omniactive Health Technologies Ltd*	Purpose
Romi Chugh *Founder - Ekon Solutions*	Talk less. Listen more. Do most.
Gaurav Loria *Group Chief Quality Officer & Head Administration*	Think big, take initiative, be decisive and persevere- you will always grow leaps & bounds!!
Hoshang Vashisht *CEO at Vashisht Group of Companies*	Believe in your product as you have believed yourself.

Nagaraja Javvaji

AVP Demand Generation & Cigniti Technologies

Close your eyes, just connect your brain with heart. Believe me, you can do wonders

QUESTION #4:
WHO ARE/WERE YOUR ROLE MODELS THAT HAVE INFLUENCED YOU IN YOUR LIFE/BUSINESS/CAREER?

SaarthakBakshi
CEO, International Fertility Centre

My role model has been Steve Jobs. He has shown me that life is a roller coaster. No matter how high you go, you will eventually come down. No matter how high the mountain is, it's only a journey. At the end of every tunnel there's always light. As long as you keep walking you will overcome all obstacles. There are others like Steve Jobs who have inspired me to continue the journey even after falling down. Failure is not the final destination, it's just a small checkpoint in the long road to success.

Ramakrishna V
Head - HR, HFFC

Animesh Kumar, he introduced me to the world of execution excellence and raising the bar like no one has ever done

PK Shrivastava
Director- Fintech , Almoayed Technologies

At different stages the Role Model changed - first it was Athlete SergaiBubka on how to keep beating your own best to become better then it was Micheal Schumacher how passion practice and excellence can bring you back to top of life even when going is tough and lastly and most longest Steve Jobs for his creativity, perfection and giving the customers what they couldn't imagine!

Pradeep Kumar Cheruvathoor
Silence Global, Chief Inspiration Officer

Lord Krishna

Pavan Verma
CEO - Redian Software

My father has put a great impact on my life, i spent my entire childhood in a small village without electricity, television and newspaper. So i was not much aware about business tycoons and influencers. Whatever i learned was from my father, he made everything from zero. I still follow his business ethics and advise. My wife also has put big impact in my life and helped in organizing the things in better way.

Apart from that i got inspiration from everyone whom i worked with right from starting my career.

Venkatachalam P
Chief People Officer of Monocept Consulting

Kapil Dev
K.V. Ramani
Dhirubhai Ambani
Narendra Modi

Lakshmiprasad Mahankali
Head of MIS & IT

Life ->My Dad & My Family
Business/Career -> my wife & all my Bosses from whom I have learned a lot of wisdom, every day is a learning day

Rohit Kilam
Head Technology, Digital

Sri Sri Ravishankar
Ratan Tata

Vijay Chaudhry
Executive Vice President, Bry Air Asia

Prof. Sumantra Ghoshal and Jack Welch

Sandhya Jathar
Head Learning & Leadership DBS bank india

Various teachers and professors in my school college .. great leaders and managers I worked with and everyone around me have taught me and inspired me

Chetan Swaroop
AVP, Pierian Services Pvt Ltd

What I have realized is that, we may have all the answers inside us, sometimes we have this vague picture of what we want to do in our personal life /career/business, but possibly certain aspects/qualities, of role model (qualities) (and maybe mentor/coaches), may help us bring it forth and push us to take action.

Rajarshi Datta
CEO, The CFO Centre India

1) My bosses Sunando Mallick, Mark Thewlis
2) Richard Branson

Mandar Sahasrabudhe
Head of IT infrastructure APAC, TUV SUD

1. Ratan Tata when i worked in Tata group of companies for his awesome leadership, immense humbleness and clarity of thoughts with vision.
2. My some of the immediate managers like KR. Murali, Sudhanshu Panse and Sanjay Joshi for their leadership capabilities.
3. Jack Ma for his amazing perseverance to build up that empire and be successful leader.
4. Some eminent regional authors and all people who taught me one or other thing everyday

Rajiv Burman
Head HR APAC Kronos

Fr. JC Prabhu, Professor at XLRI and
Dean Griffith, Founder Griffith Laboratories

Manav Sarin
Head Business Development

My father Late Mr. Ramesh sarin and My uncle you helped jubilant Pharma in India (Dr.JagmohanKhana)

Devendra Deshmukh
CEO & e-Zest Solutions Ltd.

Steve Jobs
Bill Gates
Ratan Tata

Vikram Vij
Sr. Vice President, Samsung R&D

Mahatma Gandhi
Swami Chinmayananda
Abraham Lincoln
Warren Buffet

Vinay Chataraju
VP Business Development - Ephysx Technologies

Richard Branson, Elon Musk, Sadhguru

Sandeep Gupta
Director & National Spokesperson, Expert Nutraceutical Advocacy Council

My Father will always remain my role model and Intelligent Leaders like Steve Jobs, John Mattone and Indian Prime Minister (Mr. Narendra Modi)

Anupam Sarda
AVP Product Management, HighRadius

Bill Gates/Jeff Bezos/Richard Branson

Ruchira Garg
Director, India ERC & Business Partnering, Adobe

In my career it was my first manager who did not think I was too junior to do any job. I learnt how to hire smart people and then let them do their job from him.
In life it has been my dad who has constantly reinvented himself and continues to be relevant with the times

Prakash Kumar
Head IT, BMW Group India

My parents are the leading light for me and they only taught me how to handle difficulties and remain grounded.

Arpan Banerjee
Orion Consulting Services, CEO

Ratan Tata

John Cherian
Co-founder & CEO

Sunil Handa, Professor of Entrepreneurship at IIM Ahmedabad
Narayan Murthy, Infosys Founder

Joy Banerjee
SVP & Head Learning and Development

My Mom and Dad. From the outside influence, I am influenced by Steve Jobs, Ram Charan, Warren Buffet and Wayne Dyer

Ashish Mathur
Vice President & ValueFirst Digital

Family Influencers - My Mother, Father and my Maternal Uncle.
Business -
Mr.Vishwadeep Bajaj (CEO, ValueFirst)
Late.Mr.Gagan Chadha (Co-Founder ValueFirst)

Harsha Parthasarathy
Chief Executive Officer @ Sellcraft Global Solutions

My Parents for teaching me values and integrity in life.

My first global boss at IBM, Jamie Rutledge. Who taught me to be perfect on whatever we deliver the first time itself. Also helped me to think in holistic manner and not just about our task / job.

Dr. Makarand Sawant
Senior General Manager - IT at Deepak Fertilisers And Petrochemicals Corp. Ltd.

APJ Abdul Kalam

Sudhir Gouda
Head // Strategic Alliances - Angel Broking Limited

My Parents for Life / Elon Musk, Thomas Edison & Henry Ford for Business / Bill Mcdermott for career.

Chandni Jafri
Founder and ED, SLSV (Sound and Light Social Ventures)

My father and mother, many gracious teachers and mentors who I encountered right from my early childhood to now, my colleagues and peers, customers of the brands I served and Sensei Daisaku Ikeda.

Partha Chakraborty
GM Strategic Alliances

Frankly none. But yes admire Saurav Ganguly for the

sheer gut that man showed in bringing Indian cricket upto the level where it is today.

Poornima Bushpala
Vice President Operational Risk & Control, Wells Fargo EGS India

Firstly, both my parents for their unflinching support and love to raise me and my brother and continue to do so that we can still chase our dreams and goals. Secondly, Melinda Gates and Mrs Sudha Krishna Murthy for their exceptional philanthropic work for women in technology, under privileged children, education and health.

Vineet Kumar
President - Talent Acquisition

I was always fascinated by Rakesh Sharma, the first Indian to land on moon & then Kapil Dev's as captain of Indian Cricket team winning the world cup. I always get touched by great work down by Mother Teresa and Late. Dr APJ Abdul Kalam

Dr. Sunil Pandey
Director (IT), I.T.S, Ghaziabad

My father - Try to be what you are?
Steve Jobs - Death is a beautiful thing

Ish Anand
Founder - ReliaSmart Learning Systems Pvt. Ltd. (Business Doctors India)

Jack Ma and the Dabbawalas Of Mumbai !

Tushaar Kohli
Director SUN Group

My parents, my sister, my family for my life and a number of tough bosses who made me understand hard realities of life and to learn to accept them.... Once swami on a train told me words to live by .... Be good, Do good, Be kind, Be compassionate,

Dr. Pramod Sadarjoshi
Founder & CEO, Talentsmith Consulting

1. Shri Ram Chandra of Shahajanpur, also called Babuji,
2. Swami Vivekanand
3. Mr. Ratan Tata
4. Mr. Bill Gates
5. Mr. Steve Jobs
6. MR. Steven Covey

Eric Savage
Co-founder & CEO, Unitus Capital

Nelson Mandela, Gandhi, my father, Mother Teresa

Ghanshyam Ghanshyam Singh
Director Supply Chain Management & Quality Assurance at Chai Point

- I have always been a keen observer and love to learn from anything and everything around me. I do look upto a lot of people in business like Steve jobs, Jack ma and in Sports like Muhammad Ali., but most of my learning and inspiration comes from Nature.

- The way a tree grows teaches me patience, endurance and the spirit of fighting against all odds

- The path of an asteroid teaches me the importance of exploration

- The nature of water teaches me flexibility and agility last but not the least the human spirit teaches me adaptability.

Anil Mishra
CSS Corp

Sports have always been a great influence on me and have taught me to have a positive and winning attitude. Azim Premji, Narayan Murthy, Jack Welch, Steve Jobs, Subroto Bagchi, Satya Nadella have been great business role models and had an influence on my career.

Sanjay Mahajan
Chief Information Officer, Satin Creditcare Network Ltd.

I draw inspiration from everyone, be it my peers, colleagues & subordinates. My greatest passion is to nurture people & bring out their highest potential.

Rajalingam R
Founder Director & CEO, Aberame Creative Solutions Private Limited

1. Colonel Harland Sanders, (KFC) - who taught me failures and misfortunes never stop you, keep trying always at any age.
2. AJP Abdul Kalam - who taught me how one should be humble even after reaching many heights in life and also the importance of education.

Srinath Gururajarao
Vice President / CHRO / Nexval Group

My biggest role models have been situations which were tough and needed more of everything to sail through those. Inspiration comes from even a minute creature which does its bit in sustaining the whole even when we do not understand some of them. Yes my parents, my wife and son have a been a constant "Guru's" in my journey of life in bringing smiles around and also keeping a smile on my face in the most toughest of situations.

Sunil Sonare
General Manager Sadbhav Engineering Limited

Narayan Murthy

Sourabh Tiwari
CIO, Meril group

Mr. Ratan Tata

Madhusudan Warrier
Director - Information Technology, IDFC AMC Ltd

- Mr K N Atmaramani, Former Executive Trustee - Unit Trust Of India

- Geeta M Warrier – Wife

- Mamta Joshi - My Coach

Ketan Dewan

Co-founder & CEO

Every human who brings passion to whatever they do- how my wife takes care of the kids, how my mother cooks food, how my team enables working in JLD mode (JaanLagaDengae mood- ie put your soul into whatever is your role today)

Nihar Ranjan
CEO Flashdeal

Mr.Vijay Sekhar Sharma the founder of Paytm is a source Inspiration who not being from IIT or IIM and w/o help of any co-founder has taken the company to greater heights.!

Pratik Shah
Global Head of Marketing, InstaReM

Narayan Murthy

Punit Thakkar
Shivaami Cloud Services Private Limited

I get my personal Inspiration from DadiJanki& for Business, I refer life of Bill Gates.

V.P. Prabhakaran
CTO, InfoSecTrain

Warren Buffet

Pankaj Sharma
V.P. Sales, Shaligram Infotech LLp

Mahatma Gandhi for change management, Dhirubhai, Steve Jobs-for Business, Sandip Maheswari for Life

Onais Rafiq
CEO - Fork Media India

There have been multiple, my father has been a great role model who taught me that there is no alternative to Dedication and Hard work as I moved forward role models kept changing.. I've been lucky to have had the opportunity to work with some really good people..Sanyog Jain at 160by2 which was my 1st job or Samar who founded Fork Media.

Manoj Rawat
CEO, ValueFin India

My Grandmother

Vartul Mittal
Keynote Speaker - Technology & Innovation - Ex IBM, Kotak Mahindra Bank, Coca Cola

Elon Musk is my inspiration as being a CEO of SpaceX & Tesla, he still encourages everyone to appreciate the importance to have a feedback loop, where you're constantly thinking about what you've done and how you could be doing it better. I think that's the single best piece of advice -- constantly think about how you could be doing things better and questioning yourself

Arvind Chaudhary
Co Founder at passivereferral

Understanding what is write to me and eagerness of learning made me someone who get influenced by everyone who could set learning for me in any format

Manirajjuneja
Partner, Amitojeindia

Guru Nanak

Sandipan Chattopadhyay
CEO and MD, Xelpmoc Design and Tech Limited

VergheseKurien, Dr GV Nageshwara Rao and VSS Mani

Rakesh Bhambhani
Chief Business Officer - Clove Technologies Pvt Ltd

Many Business Leaders have Influenced my Life. Be a Sponge, Absorb as much as you can or want.

Sharjeel Siddiqui
Head of Marketing / LogiNext

Nikola Tesla, Stephen Hawking, Jack Ma, Elon Musk

Jayprakash Vasdewani
CEO, Latitude Technolabs Pvt ltd

My life changed when I came to USA for studies. I worked for a research lab as well did odd jobs. Every boss encouraged me. Paul Bohjanen, my first Boss always encouraged and gave me room to grow. I learnt from him how to let person grow under you. I have tried to do the same with all of my team.

Subash Franklin
StratSprint

Clayton M Christensen of Harvard Business School

LEADING WITH EXCELLENCE

Sachin Deshpande
Co-Founder & CEO

Swami Vivekanand

Chakravarthy Murugesan
General Manager, Net 4 India Ltd

Richard Branson and Steve Jobs

Amit Dua
CEO, Signity Solutions

Robin Sharma - Got Initial inspiration from his writing
Napoleon Hill - His classic "Think & Grow Rich" acted as catalyst to plunge into entrepreneurship.
Raman Roy, Chairman & MD - Quattro - His journey as pioneer in Indian BPO is inspiring

Sankar Bora
Founder & COO @Dealshare

Mark Zuckerberg, mainly for two reasons - For opening up the Social angle for business and starting up so young.

Hitesh Gossain
Managing Director, Onspon.com

Richard Branson : Eccentric but focussed
Steve Jobs : Sharp vision

Sanjaya Mariwala
Omniactive Health Technologies Ltd

There are so many; no one or two. You meet a lot of people in this world, and one should. You learn from everyone, if you observe and are keen. You can learn from everyone's success and failures, so there is no one person who can teach you everything.

Romi Chugh
Founder - Ekon Solutions

I've never really had a role model, but I did feel inspired by Stephen Hawking - that disability or the lack of ability should be the only fuel to fire your dreams.

Gaurav Loria
Group Chief Quality Officer & Head Administration

I believe admiration is all about loving with the mind, imbibe the best and still have your own style. Many leaders have existed who have given so much to the world in their own unique ways. Every individual teaches us something – a virtue, an act, an experience or a skill.

There are many- to name a few- Sir Richard Branson, Ms Indra Nooyi, Steve Jobs & Mark Zuckerberg, leadership spirit of M S Dhoni and financial outlook of Warren Buffett.

Hoshang Vashisht
CEO at Vashisht Group of Companies

Warren buffet, Jeff Bezos, Ratan Tata, Jack ma, Elon Musk & Mark Zuckerberg

Nagaraja Javvaji
AVP Demand Generation & Cigniti Technologies

Sashi Reddi - Founder & Managing Partner SRI Capital
Sanju Pillai - CEO MovingDNeedle
Sai Chintala - President Innominds
My wife and friends

Nidhin Chandra Mohan
Director, SayOne Technologies Private Limited

Ayn Rand

Pranav Shandilya
Founder and CEO- 12th July Ventures

Steve Jobs

Siddharth Hosangadi
Vice President - Sales, Uniphore Software Systems

H.H. Radhanath Swami - ISKCON Guru
Ranjan Das - Late MD of SAP India
Alok Srivastava - MD CISCO
Hrishikesh Mafatlal - Chairman Mafatlal Industries

Gauraav Thakar
QualityKiosk, Vice President

David Ben Gurion, Steve Jobs, Bill Gates, Mukesh Ambani, Jack Ma, Golda Meir, Narendra Modi, Genghis Khan

Akshar Peerbhoy
COO - MAA Communications

Steve Jobs. Richard Branson

Srivibhavan Balaram
Managing Director, Vocera Communications India Pvt Ltd

Stephen Covey
Eric Schmidt
Vikram Shah - He was MD of Novell India and later MD at NetApp India

Krishna Prasad
Interaction One Solutions Private Limited

Bill Gates and many of my managers specially in my early years who have shaped my career.

Srikanth Appana
Co Founder & CTO, ASAP

Steve Wozniak for technical brillance
Jack Welch for his radical leadership
Abdul Kalam for his simplicity and hard work

Praveen Kumar Kalbhavi
CMD & CEO - Novigo Solutions Inc

Mr. Narayana Murthy (Founder of Infosys)

Flight Lieutenant At Kishore
Chief Entrepreneurial Officer, Vidhya Sangha

My Father who told me to be like Happy Prince[Oscar Wild-fiction] and mom who inspired me to be tolerant to all religions and fight against social ills including illiteracy and dowry stigmas

Ashesh Shah
CEO - Fusion Informatics Limited

Amitabh Bachchan, Bill Gates, Sardar Vallabhbhai Patel, Steve Jobs, Mahatama Gandhi

Anjani Madhavi
Vice President - Envestnet /Yodlee

Robin Sharma, Satya Nadella, Mahatria Ra

Dhruv Pandey
CEO (Maxosys Limited)

My Role model is Late Sh. Dhiru Bhai Ambani.

Vikas Chadha
Executive Director and CFO Berggruen Hotels Pvt ltd

Was influenced by JRD Tata, Steve Jobs, Narayan Murthy

Kalyan Acharya
Business Development Head-Global Sales at Yudiz Solutions Pvt.Ltd.

Mr. Bharat Patel, Co-Founder of Yudiz Solutions Pvt. Ltd.

Madhuri Mandaogade
CEO, HumaneBITS

I get inspired to see women leaders across different fields. Indra Nooyi is definitely one of them.
Dr. Doreen Granpeesheh, CEO and Founder of Center for Autism and Related Disorders has been my role model since last many years.

Manav Jeet
MD & CEO

Not really a role model but three books that have inspired me are: Total Recall, Xiaomi Way & Dare to Dream. The common theme in all these books is their persistence to pursue the goal despite adverse situation which laid them to great success & role model themselves for entire world

Sonal Jain
HR Director Johnson and Johnson

My role model has been Steve Jobs. He has shown me that life is a roller coaster. No matter how high you go, you will eventually come down. No matter how high the mountain is, it's only a journey. At the end of every tunnel there's always light. As long as you keep walking you will overcome all obstacles. There are others like Steve Jobs who have inspired me to continue the journey even after falling down. Failure is not the final destination, it's just a small checkpoint in the long road to success.

Sharmilaa Rajesh Kannan
Vice President_Learning& Development

My mother largely influenced me as a person, I think I have got her never say die attitude. she always said no matter what life throws at you, you will always figure out a way to handle it with a smile. believe you me, its been my guiding mantra in toughest of the situations. one more person who is off late making me learn new things is Nishtha, my 6 year old daughter. I have learned persistence and curiosity from her. her never ending questions and the energizer bunny attitude baffles me yet it makes me realize that curiosity keeps the learner in me alive. she doesnt rest till she finds answers to her questions. if i buy time from her to answer something, she will approach her father or try a voice search on google since she is yet learning to spell. its amazing to see her being resourceful in getting what she wants.

In career i am greatly influenced by Herb keheller, the Co-founder of southwest airlines. I simply admire his ability to think out of the box, be unconventional yet mean business.

QUESTION #5: WHAT IS YOUR MESSAGE (IN ONE PARAGRAPH) TO THE WORLD?

- The world owes no one anything, it was here first. Don't waste time pondering over what others should have done. In the larger scheme of things, we occupy a very small frame of space and time. Focus on what you can do to make it worth it.

Ruchira Garg
Director, India ERC & Business Partnering, Adobe

- If you want to change the world, go do it!

Eric Savage
Co-founder & CEO,
Unitus Capital

- look or force others to change so that we get the best. If we want change in others, start with yourself, BE THE CHANGE YOU WANT TO SEE IN THE WORLD. Lead by example. Teach others with our positive experiences. Be the change! We need help, to become better self-aware beings, and discover our true potential. Be Human
- Learn to accept that one will not get everything. Not getting something is not the end, it is just a completion.
- Don't go blindly and persuade others for validation of your belief.
- Spend some time with the ones you love the most. Your Parents, Spouse, Best Friends - Talk to them, Love them and will never calculate their amount of happiness by this. Always remember— Parents are the only ones obligated to love you; You have to earn love and respect from rest of the world.

Madhusudan Warrier
Director - Information Technology, IDFC AMC Ltd

- Don't compare. Be the original version of yourself and that is only possible with constantly observing the motive behind your actions. With the new found you, give your one way video interviews on TALOCITY Touchless Talent for jobs at our client locations across India & Asia. The world of HR is becoming TOUCHLESS and very proud to be part of that movement.

Ketan Dewan
Co-founder & CEO

- Strive for excellence in whatever you do . Do what you like with passion and positivity . Be humble , help yourself and others to Succeed .Life is full of adventures and enjoy it.

Mandar Sahasrabudhe
Head of IT Infrastructure APAC, TUV SUD

- By giving your time and support to help others succeed you will build better relationships and value.

Rajiv Burman
Head HR APAC
Kronos

- Love your self first... that's how you can improve the world and love others.

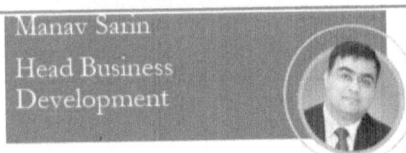

Manav Sarin
Head Business Development

- If you want to scale your business or your career, you need to constantly ask -Can I get this task done without doing the work myself?

You need to focus on the big picture and delegate tasks. Don't be a control freak. Mentor, Guide, coach but don't do the tasks yourself.

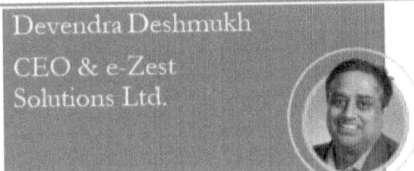

Devendra Deshmukh
CEO & e-Zest Solutions Ltd.

- The world is a manifestation of our collective thoughts. So think big and think positive. Let everyone's positive energy and the light of wisdom guide us through the journey of life.

Vikram Vij
Sr. Vice President, Samsung R&D

- Entrepreneur is an ever evolving process that compels you to unlearn many things on order to adapt to the new role. I spent more than 25 years in the corporate world. However, as an entrepreneur, the job on other side of the table is very different. Therefore, always be open to unlearn to learn new things as adaptability is the key to operate in dynamic scenario.

Manav Jeet
MD & CEO

- Profit and Purpose both are important to succeed as a Good Human Being !!

Sachin Deshpande
Co-Founder & CEO

- Live the moment....
Just believe that all the dots would connect in future when you look at backwards...Keep moving

Chakravarthy Murugesan
General Manager ,Net 4 India Ltd

- Stay Hungry, Stay Foolish - Entrepreneur makes quick decision and is not afraid of making mistakes. If you are a budding entrepreneur or aspirant to be an entrepreneur, don't bogged down by if & buts, just make a decision & move forward. More than success or charm of achievement, an entrepreneur is blessed to generate more employment & help make this world a better place.

Amit Dua
CEO, Signity Solutions

- Perseverance is the key to success. Even if one fails, there is always a way ahead, and a lot of learning, which should never stop. The path to success is not always swift, and even Rome wasn't built in a day.

Sankar Bora
Founder & COO
@Dealshare

- We have gotten one life to live. We can choose to live for ourself or to create a bigger impact. What you do with every second of life shapes how you affect the world ; and no amount of self gratification will ever make up for it. Live to create impact.

Hitesh Gossain
Managing Director,
Onspon.com

- Have purpose in your life, build your self a set of core values, practice them and sleep with a clean conscience. Enjoy what you do and have fun in your work. If not change it. Be ready always to accept change and other views.

Sanjaya Mariwala
Omniactive Health
Technologies Ltd

- We always want to start something but never do, for whatever reasons. The only way I know how to do is to do. Rather have the satisfaction of trying and failing, than to have the regret of never doing at all.

Romi Chugh
Founder - Ekon Solutions

- A healthy work life balance is as critical as breathing. The stress today can hurt relationships, health and overall happiness. The balance is never defined, never enough or not always equal. But we need to work towards the same and ensure that we achieve (at work) and enjoy (with family & friends). Life is too short and we should believe in leaving a legacy behind so that people remember you for the king size life that you lived.

Gaurav loria
Group Chief Quality Officer & Head Administration

- "We Humans are bounded by the greatness of Greed. Lets Greed for Knowledge."

Our one purpose of existence is to build something which is beneficial for the whole humanity & mankind. We need to love & help each other to grow, learn, adapt, evolve & transcendence into the reality. The deeper in your heart you live, the clearer the path becomes. How can one of us be happy if all the other ones are sad. UBUNTU in xhosa culture means 'i am because we are'

If you do what you like with 100% involvement, what you dont like, you must do with 200% involvement. Thats Breaking Limitations 'Sadhguru'

Hoshang Vashisht
CEO at Vashisht
Group of Companies

- If you spend proper time with you and your family members. You are the most successful person in the world. Life is very sweet and short, let's enjoy every moment :-)

Nagaraja Javvaji
AVP Demand
Generation & Cigniti
Technologies

- People under value their potential in general. Humans are capable of doing a lot more when they put their heart into it. We should target to reach our maximum potential and solve the world problems efficiently. We should build our foundation strong and constantly question our own beliefs and keep improving that.

Vinay Chataraju
VP Business Development - Ephysx Technologies

- Live with Passion & Purpose, you will reach your dream. Live to create impact on Heart, Soul and Mind of Society

Sandeep Gupta
Director & National Spokesperson, Expert Nutraceutical Advocacy Council

- It takes lot of courage to take on the entire opposition you have in life but by thinking in a simple manner and being you (or Transparent/Truthful) you can win over any situation in life.

Lakshmiprasad Mahankali
Head of MIS & IT

- Love your work

Rohit Kilam
Head Technology, Digital

- We as human being should always believe in changes and we must work for the human development in all kind for upliftment of the society with innovation and knowledge building. We also take care that resources to be utilized and shared equally among all the live creatures of the earth with protection of our environment.

Sunil Sonare
General Manager
Sadbhav Engineering Limited

- Reading is key to gaining wisdom, but beyond raw knowledge and information, a good book can inspire you with the new possibilities and ideas it presents (with new world)… and empower you to come up with your own.

Sourabh Tiwari
CIO, Meril group

- I have lived by this lesson "Whatever it takes" from the time I can recollect, and it had always opened up new opportunities when I was least expecting any. So here are some thoughts for two sets of folks I interact a lot with, employees who are fresh from college and people who have been working for some time now.

For the fresh ones I will say try different things, remain flexible, open to change, I have seen too many people early in the career not wanting to try new things or put in all their effort even when the organization is giving them an opportunity to do so, it is a great idea to do whatever it takes to fulfill your responsibilities. You never know what new opportunities will come your way.

For the ones who have been working for some time now can relate to this as well, you will not like or enjoy everything that comes as part of your responsibilities. But it is imperative that you do it with all your commitment to keeping the larger picture in mind and when there are more critical or complex projects the organization will reach out to you because they trust you to deliver, not because you are an expert in some field but because of your commitment to "whatever it takes".

AVP Product Management, HighRadius

- The world is a beautiful place, unfortunately, humans are consuming it for themselves and destroying it. Our future generations will curse us for this callousness and greed. Let's save the planet and the human kind. My only advise is " live and let live".

Prakash Kumar
Head IT, BMW Group India

- Its never too late to start

Arpan Banerjee
Orion Consulting Services, CEO

- The race and aspiration of professionals to become a leader of masses than having any meaning purpose in professional life has only created corporate snollygoster, beware of these managers, they are cancerous to growth and radical performance.

Vijay Chaudhry
Executive Vice President, Bry Air Asia

- Just live and let live be humble and thankful.. don't harm people and other beings take care of your self and your ecosystem.. learn from mistakes and live everyday to make the tomorrow better for you and beings around..let there be light for all .

Sandhya Jathar
Head Learning & Leadership DBS Bank
India

- One can always correct themselves by searching for the truths, without making it an ego issue. That way, creating a better world view becomes a lot easier.

Chetan Swaroop
AVP, Pierian Services Pvt Ltd

- To be able to do what you want, when you want is what one should strive for. Work hard, be focussed and be passionate in your work to achieve that. There is no short cut to success.

Rajarshi Datta
CEO, The CFO Centre India

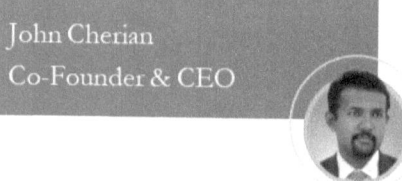

- You have only one life. You either use it to live your dream or help others live their dreams. Either way, use it well.

John Cherian
Co-Founder & CEO

- The journey of thousand miles starts with a single step and after that it is whole journey of exploration, learnings, experience and should never stop, until one is rested for this life. Keep the modesty and realization that what we have today is because of what we did yesterday and a lot depends on what we do in the present for our future.

Joy Banerjee
SVP & Head Learning and Development

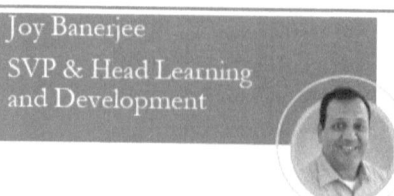

- Believe in yourself! Would like to share Wolfgang Riebe quote "No one is perfect - that's why pencils have erasers."

Ashish Mathur
Vice President
&ValueFirst Digital

- First of all explore and exploit your abilities. Everyone in this world have unique capabilities, you can do wonders!! Values and Integrity is another important trait anyone should not compromise.

  Believe in yourself, there will be ups and downs in career and life, but we have to overcome those and it is possible only by you.

  One life, live it fully !!

Harsha Parthasarathy
Chief Executive Officer @ Sellcraft Global Solutions

- Question everything till you're convinced.

Dr. Makarand Sawant
Senior General Manager - IT at Deepak Fertilisers And Petrochemicals Corp. Ltd.

- It's a game of perspective going on out there. You choose your point of views and destiny in return chooses you for that. Be relentless in pursuing your goals, for life without goals is a body without soul. No one ever said it was going to be easy, for "Easy" forever has been overrated. Stay focused, stay motivated and inspire others in joining your cause. Like Jobs says it "Management is about persuading people to do things they don't wanna do, while leadership is inspiring people to do things, they never thought they could."

Sudhir Gouda
Head || Strategic Alliances - Angel Broking Limited

- I believe in Triple Bottom line - People, Planet and Profit - successful businesses of the future will have to rest on these three pillars. Ignoring any one will most definitely result in the business failing. Understanding and managing Triple Bottom line will create highly profitable businesses who will have a lasting impact on the world.

Chandni Jafri
Founder and ED,
SLSV (Sound and Light Social Ventures)

- One world vision is to make our world a Happy place to live. By encouraging countries to measure prosperity through happiness index and not limit only to the per captia income or GDP. Motivate leaders to understand grass root problems of the people and lead through innovation and higher emotional intelligence to address uncertainities that prevail in the eco system and create a powerful social impact for nation building.

Poornima Bushpala
Vice President
Operational Risk & Control, Wells Fargo
EGS India

- As human beings on earth, we must accept the fact that god has given sunlight to everyone - plants, animals and of-course us. Everyone in this world should get equal opportunity to grow, learn and be happy. Do not hurt and lead a peaceful life.

Vineet Kumar
Vice President - Talent Acquisition

- Life is never easy. It has spikes of good and bad experiences both. Keep your nerves under control when you are going through tough time or with phase of happiness & success. And always try to remain a good human being. You will come across all the odds.

Dr. Sunil Pandey
Director (IT), I.T.S, Ghaziabad

- Whatever life throws at you, even if it hurts you, just be strong and fight through it. Remember, strong walls shake but never collapse

Ish Anand
Founder - ReliaSmart Learning Systems Pvt. Ltd. (Business Doctors India)

- 406 Technology Apartments
24 I P Extension
Delhi 110092

Tushaar Kohli
Director SUN Group

- Practice one H and 5 cs :

  1. Heartfulness & clarity
  2. Creation
  3. Courageousness
  4. Connectedness
  5. Compassion

Dr. Pramod Sadarjoshi
Founder & CEO, Talentsmith Consulting

- We are a bunch of people on a solid sphere going around a ball of fire much bigger than us, in the middle of nowhere, with more questions about life than answers, uncertainty is inevitable and one should get comfortable with it.

  There will always be some questions we will have but it is important to take the first step, no matter what, if not by sight, then by faith and things will fall in place.

Ghanshyam
Ghanshyam Singh
Director Supply Chain Management & Quality Assurance at Chai Point

- Enjoy life to the fullest with a positive mindset and a learning attitude. As Steve Jobs said, You can only Connect the Dots looking backwards, hence give your 100% commitment and effort to the role you are playing know and once you look backwards, you will realize God has created a beautiful path for each one of us. Enjoy life to the fullest with a positive mindset and a learning attitude. As Steve Jobs said, You can only Connect the Dots looking backwards, hence give your 100% commitment and effort to the role you are playing know and once you look backwards, you will realize God has created a beautiful path for each one of us.

Anil Mishra
CSS Corp

- We should have a mission in life, have passion to achieve our dreams, never give up in adversity & always stay grounded when we achieve success.

Sanjay Mahajan

Chief Information Officer || Satin Creditcare Network Ltd.

- Everyone life is different and cannot give any life advice to others as we do not have control over everything in own life. However, we have control over something in life. Choose what you can control in life and wear a smile which is always in your control. One of the most important things in life is to be polite and respect for others. Don't worry about others criticism or their opinions as it is not the fact. I think the difference of opinion are healthy and make the world more interesting. Believe in you and move with it and live life happily.

Rajalingam R

Founder Director & CEO, Aberame Creative Solutions Private Limited

- A world is a whole which is conceived as individual unique's with artificial boundaries defined, a human mind and actions are full of great possibilities to navigate and create a better tomorrow and making today a more meaningful journey, make it count and let that be the best of what we stand for and give.

Srinath Gururajarao
Vice President | CHRO | Nexval Group

- Life is a wonderland of aspiration and ambition. This wonderland becomes beautiful when it has surroundings (context) and connections (people, objects). All human beings interact with these surroundings and people based on multiple energies and aura they radiate and absorb from others. The degree of our relationships, networks, connections are an outcome of these energies and aura of ourselves and others. The magic happens in these moments of interactions. Create that magic every moment for yourself and for others. There is only one opportunity to create the magic moment which creates the wonderland complete.

Sonal Jain
HR Director Johnson and Johnson

- I want to tel everyone that you need to embrace failure. No matter how hard you try, life would put you down and whenever you get knocked down, I need you to get back up. There is no easy solution to success. It only comes to those who keep trying and persevering all day and night long. Success comes before work only in a dictionary. In real life every it's a long & tedious journey which will take a toll on you. Only those people who cant rise beyond and challenge the status quo will eventually succeed. My message to the world is that don't be afraid of failure. Everyone of us is meant to fail sooner or later. People who question "what if" will never be able to succeed. If I have been given 1 life, I want to live it without fear and at the end of my journey, I want to say that yes I did try and that was soul-fulfilling.

SaarthakBakshi
CEO, International Fertility Centre

- I am convinced that this world is a great place because I truly believe in the goodness in everyone. Together we can make this a happy place if we remember this when are faced with a conflict situation. My mantra is "Inner peace leads to world peace"

Ramakrishna V
Head - HR, HFFC

- Message to my fellow human beings is change one thing at a time and start it from yourself. Dont wait for things to happen, just do it. Show love and care without hesitation for it returns manifolds at unexpected time. Try making a difference in someone's life always. Dont be selfish, use resources cautiously for we dont want our children and generations to come suffer for our follies. Plant a tree, sing a song, hike up a mountain, fulfill your bucketlist cause time wont wait. "There is only one life and if you do things right, just one life is enough"

Sharmilaa Rajesh Kannan

Vice President_Learning& Development

- Life is short but interesting journey. Everyone around you have got an opinion but honestly it does not matter. What really matters is what you believe in , what your passion is. Do what you love and love what you do. Dont either follow what everyone does or do anything just for making money. If you can follow your heart and pursue your dream you would feel the satisfaction no money can buy you. However its important to follow the right path and have clear conscious that would guarantee you peaceful sleep irrespective of whatever world may think of you! if you ever plan to start a business look for passion for idea in your founding team choose the people you sourrpund yourself- nothing but the best!Lastly stay humble stay grounded and stay focussed on big picture!

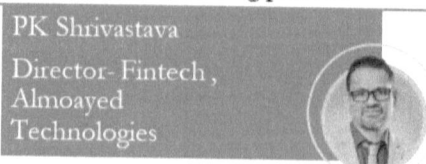

PK Shrivastava

Director- Fintech , Almoayed Technologies

- The World is One. Thought creates a sense of separation.

Pradeep Kumar Cheruvathoor

Silence Global, Chief Inspiration Officer

- There is lot to learn from the past and people around you. You should take a lesson from your mistakes and try not repeat it again. Keep your hunger alive and zeal with you. There is long way to go.

Pavan Verma

CEO, Redian software

- Do work and contribute for your nation. Love all the living being. Care for mother Earth.

Venkatachalam P

Chief People Officer of Monocept Consulting

- The big challenge is raising funds, This is something that will happen with you and every other startups out there. It's not as easy as it seems to raise capital for your venture. People who put in the money early, usually the angels, they want to see if they are betting on the right set of talent at right time and you exit plan for them too..

Nihar Ranjan
CEO Flashdeal

- In the quest of 'life', don't quit living.

Pratik Shah
Global Head of Marketing, InstaReM

- Think, who will cry when you die has been my way of working. So any work I engage in, I would think if it makes any positive change in the life of the person I am connected with. If yes, then it is my way.

Punit Thakkar
Shivaami Cloud Services Private Limited

- Trust your strengths and keep learning from everyone in life. To stay ahead of the game, train your inner powers not to miss any chance to grab any opportunity. Misfortune and destiny are the words for those who do not trust their abilities. We all are able in some or the other ways. Only, the need is to identify that ability and strengthen it with learning more and stay focused to your goals.

V.P. Prabhakaran
CTO, InfoSecTrain

- Help each other to create better world for coming generations.

Pankaj Sharma
V.P. Sales, Shaligram Infotech LLp

- Focus on doing the right thing, don't let yourself get lost in "doing" that you lose touch with what really matters.

  In todays day and age its criminal to take things for granted.

Onais Rafiq
CEO - Fork Media
India

- Life is full of unlimited possibilities. We rarely experience and explore most of it.

Manoj Rawat
CEO, ValueFin India

- When you're aiming to improve on a particular product or service, management style, business process or something else, your best move is to intentionally not be the smartest person in the room; you hire people brighter than you, add humble pie to your diet, and solicit consistent feedback to improve yourself and the business.

VARTUL MITTAL
Keynote Speaker - Technology & Innovation - Ex IBM, Kotak Mahindra Bank, Coca Cola

- Passion and perseverance can help you achieve pretty much anything. The stamina and the will to keep on going day after day is probably the key. High IQ, luck, fancy degrees, the traditional milestones- are perhaps not as helpful as passion and persistence. You have to keep going through non-glamorous days with the same amount of passion. If you are able to do it, success will come!

Madhuri Mandaogade
- CEO, HumaneBITS

- I am not sure what is the audience of this message But if you are a entrepreneur Start loving challenges More you face them more it makes you a refined problem solved.

  Arvind Chaudhary
  Co Founder at passivereferral

- Be completely obsessed about giving others a better experience, a better life, a better feeling. When you keep doing this consistently you suddenly discover you reach a stage where people start to notice, and get inspired.

  Manirajjuneja
  Partner, Amitojeindia

- 2b Crown Aura
  Jakkur Plantation Road
  Bengaluru 560064

Sandipan Chattopadhyay

CEO and MD, Xelpmoc Design and Tech Limited

- It is always about adding Value.
  Adding Value to the stake holders who are associated with what you do be it at work or be at home.
  Firmly believe: Play for Long term, Be passionate, Always be objective, Constantly seek for more information and then ACT to add value.

Rakesh Bhambhani

Chief Business Officer - Clove Technologies Pvt Ltd

- There always are 3 types of people in this world, 1- Those who want to command 2- Those who want to be commanded 3- Those who don't like to command or be commanded.
It is very important that we introspect at a very early stage of our career and identify which category we fall under, and, the only thing which would help you identify the right category is by "Stop lying to yourself". If you are not a leader then don't try to be one, cause you will be bad at it. Similarly, if you cannot follow any leader then it's perfectly fine, you are a lone ranger, play by your rules. Remember, no matter which category you fall under, dedication and focus in what you do and how you do it, will make define your success.

Sharjeel Siddiqui
Head of Marketing | LogiNext

- Do what you love, there is no point in doing something you hate, it will completely burn you. Focus on your work, money will follow.

Jayprakash Vasdewani
CEO, Latitude Technolabs Pvt ltd

- Realise that life is not a fair game. There will be ups and downs which sometimes will be out of your control, but that doesn't mean you should not work towards a goal. Keep doing everything that for that goal and leave the rest to the universe. You will have a sense of peace and satisfaction that you did your best.

Subash Franklin

StratSprint

- Never complain, Practise Gratitude, Be thankful every day.

Nidhin Chandra Mohan

Director, SayOne Technologies Private Limited

- Make wise choices, live life king size!

Pranav Shandilya

Founder and CEO - 12th July Ventures

- The only real problem today in the world is a lack of (genuine) God consciousness, and the only real solution is genuine God consciousness. Today due to the utter godlessness in society, there is unfettered greed, apathy, violence and selfishness at the individual, family, society as well as country level. Those who are genuinely God conscious are more sensitive to human beings, other living entities, recognize that Nature is a gift from God and hence don't defile it, do their duties sincerely to the best of their abilities as a service to God, and contribute back to society.

  Hence, rather than trying to work on a million things, if everyone worked on this one thing - become more God conscious - we will have probably a better world to live in.

Siddharth Hosangadi
Vice President - Sales,
Uniphore Software Systems

- Put all your energy in exploring it's depth - give it all you got - blood, sweat and tears. When you finally reach your goal you will realize that your true victory was the journey itself.

Gauraav Thakar
QualityKiosk, Vice President

- Believe in humanity, believe in a higher power and most importantly believe in the power of knowledge

Akshar Peerbhoy
COO - MAA Communications

- Strive for excellence in anything that you do. Always work towards doing what you love to do. Get rid of your ego - it is the only thing that can derail you. In the different situations that life throws at you, always acknowledge your emotions but never respond emotionally. Respond only when you have stepped away from your emotions. Help others in whatever way you can.

Srivibhavan Balaram
Managing Director,
Vocera Communications India Pvt Ltd

- Identify what is important for you, prioritise life goals, aim high and follow your own path.

Krishna Prasad
Interaction One Solutions Private Limited

- Always compete yourself! come out of your comfort zone challenge new opportunities and break your monotonous careers.

  Always keep learning, It may be personal or professional learning should never stop, this will help to overcome situations.

  Make decisions only based on data and facts, ensure any decision taken is supported by evidences and always make relevant stakeholders should be involved while framing the solution or taking decisions. Always it should be "WE" but not "I"

Srikanth Appana
Co Founder & CTO, ASAP

- Enjoy what you are doing and do what you enjoy, but not at the cost of others. There is no end to learning and keep learning from everyone and everything around. Do love & respect all around. Be compassionate, humble & Simple in life. All the best to everyone.

Praveen Kumar Kalbhavi
CMD & CEO - Novigo Solutions Inc

- Global Warming Awareness, Education for All, Innovation in EV, Batteries for several new vehicular technologies, Drones and connected car, V2V,V2X,D2D. Use of AI,ML and Deep Learning in education for preparing youth strictly as per Bloom's Taxonomy

Kishore
Chief Entrepreneurial officer, Vidhya Sangha

- Share yourself, Expand your boundaries, Have a generous heart and Focus on Being.

Ashesh Shah
CEO - Fusion Informatics Limited

- All of the world's evolution - we owe it to those few, who didn't know what 'impossible' means, who were out to do things most of the mediocre folks didn't even imagine.

  Become one of those few - go all out to do things that will change the world - forever! If Nelson Mandela could bring an end to apartheid despite being in prison for 27 years, imagine what you & I can do - having the freedom to be able to easily make a difference!
  Like Mahatma Gandhi said - "Be the change you want to see in the world!"

Anjani Madhavi
Vice President - Envestnet | Yodlee

- My message to the world is Worship Nature and contribute for environment protection.
Life is very short. We all are actors and actress in this life drama. We are alone. We have no brought anything and we will not take anything after death. We are passer by and only we are creating relation during our journeying.
Conserve natural resources and follow the path of sustainable development. Have faith and create faith as faith is the powerful weapon to solve every problem. Create world brotherhood so that there will be peace in the world.

Dhruv Pandey
CEO (Maxosys Limited)

- Do what you enjoy doing it will make the journey to success sweeter. There would be constraints and frustrations in your path to success but they will pass as you travel through your journey. Enjoy the journey as true happiness is in the journey, interactions and people you meet and final destination is just a certificate of having completed the marathon of life

Vikas Chadha

Executive Director and CFO Berggruen Hotels Pvt ltd

- I would like to give a message to the tech community that though technology has revolutionized our lives, it has now become very important for us to judge the pros and cons of every solution or invention very smartly. This will help us create a better future without having any adverse effects on mankind. We will need to give a proper consultation and educate everyone about our products related to modern technologies so that they can be put to a right use. At Yudiz, we aim to provide these kinds of solutions through our consultative approach.

Kalyan Acharya

Business Development Head-Global Sales at Yudiz Solutions Pvt.Ltd.

LEADING WITH EXCELLENCE

BOOK RAAM AS A SPEAKER AT YOUR EVENTS

FOR OVER A DECADE, Raam Anand has been educating, entertaining, motivating, and inspiring business owners, entrepreneurs, startups, VP and C-level executives, coaches, consultants, advisors, experts and professionals build their platforms, amplify their message and become thought-leaders, authorities and celebrity influencers.

He'll guide any audience step-by-step how to build and grow any businesses with bestselling books, online marketing, social media, mobile, and product creation strategies that are proven to work.

His origin story includes his transformation over the last two decades, going from an under-privileged, middle-class family kid to becoming the top leader and coach around the world with no backing, no investment and nothing more than a shirt on his back.

After successfully building multiple businesses and brands across North America and India, Raam can share relevant, actionable strategies that anyone can use—even if they're starting from scratch.

His unique style inspires, empowers, and entertains audiences while giving them the tools and strategies they need and want to get seen and heard to build and grow successful sustainable brands and businesses.

Raam has trained, coached, spoken to and helped Billionaires, Olympic coaches, Top Executives, Experts, Entrepreneurs and Professionals in various industries across the globe.

RAAM SPEAKS ON A VARIETY OF TOPICS SUCH AS:

- High Performance
- Influence and Persuasion
- Rapid Book Publishing
- Personal Branding
- Innovation and Product Creation
- Speaking/Selling from the Stage
- Strategic Marketing
- Selling Like Superstars

HOW TO BOOK:

Email info@stardomalliance.com or call +1(302)-504-4257 (USA) or 99648-12292 (India)

[FREE BOOK] - Get a free copy of the book "Write Now" by Raam Anand, and see how you too can become a bestselling author EVEN if you have never written anything before!

Own book is the #1 marketing strategy used by successful and highly respected leaders all over the world. You too can become an author.. and create 10x better opportunities for your life and business.

Don't miss this one!

Click below or visit and claim your free copy before it's too late (just cover s&h, get it shipped to anywhere in India):

http://StardomBooks.com

Even though the results of becoming an author is incredible, writing a book can be a frustrating, painful process... especially if it's your first time. Raam has watched people struggle through this process (for years) the hard way, and he has also taught 1,000's of people to breeze through this process the easy way. Which way will you choose?

Here Are A Few Of The Things You'll Learn Inside This FREE Book...

+ Why should I write a book right now? - pg. 1

+ How a book turns attention into MONEY and how to create it FAST? - pg. 11

+ 6 Goals for writing a book and how to choose the BEST one? - pg. 27

+ How to become an author EVEN if you are not a professional writer - pg. 33

+ Creating a bestselling book EVEN if English is NOT your first language - pg. 39

+ My SECRET strategy for BUSY people who do not have time to write a book - pg. 43

+ Everything you should know about ISBN and why you should care about it? - pg. 47

+ Why shouldn't you SELF-PUBLISH your book (if you ignore this it will take you YEARS to write your book!) -pg. 51

+ How to choose what to WRITE about in your first book? (this insight can save you a lot of embarrassment later) - pg. 59

+ Who will read your book?...this tip alone will help you start right and keep you from writing a book that no one reads! -pg. 63

+ Figuring out how much knowledge or wisdom is REALLY required for writing a book -pg. 67

+ Using your book as a MARKETING weapon (HINT: the real returns from a book are in the back-end!) -pg. 75

+ How to choose the RIGHT coach to help you become an internationally published author -pg. 83

+ How to earn maximum ROYALTIES from your book (the wrong publisher choice can set you up for a huge loss) -pg. 91

+ Why should I publish RIGHT NOW (don't let this chance slip through your fingers) -pg. 93

+ Choosing whether to publish locally or going for a WORLDWIDE release (giving wings to your message) -pg. 136

+ How to build your own EXPERT-EMPIRE around your thoughts using a book? - pg. 117

+ How to use a book to start or grow your professional speaking career -pg. 119

+ Self-Assessment - goal attainment and neuro-science based test on whether you can actually become an author! - pg 135

Here's What To Do Next...

Like I mentioned before, this book is FREE. All we ask is that you cover the small shipping and handling fee of just ₹49 only to get this book delivered to your address.

Get your free copy here:
http://StardomBooks.com

LEADING WITH EXCELLENCE